know how to KEEP SALTWATER FISHES

by William P. Braker
**Director: Shedd Aquarium,
Chicago, Illinois**

Earl Schneider, editor

THE PET LIBRARY LTD

THE PET LIBRARY LTD ®

The Pet Library Ltd, subsidiary of Sternco Industries, Inc., 600 South Fourth Street, Harrison, N.J. Exclusive Canadian Distributor: Hartz Mountain Pet Supplies Limited, 1125 Talbot Street, St. Thomas, Ontario, Canada.

Exclusive United Kingdom Distributor: The Pet Library (London) Ltd, 30 Borough High Street, London S.E.1.

PRINTED IN THE NETHERLANDS

ISBN 0-87826-720-4

CONTENTS

1 Introduction

This book was written primarily for the hobbyist who has had experience keeping fresh-water fishes, but is a neophyte in the sea-water field. I have tried to present basic information that I think is important in establishing a salt-water system.

The fishes listed and pictured here have been chosen from hundreds available to the salt-water hobbyist. They are almost always available and relatively inexpensive. There are a few exceptions such as the Moorish idol, but most of the species can readily be found on one dealer's list or another.

The going will not be easy, and you should be prepared to lose fish, but do not become discouraged. Remember that there are many dealers, importers, and pioneers in the saltwater field who suffered losses for years in order to make the hobby what it is today. The chapter on fish diseases will help you recognize and treat some of the common ailments but it cannot cover the whole field. Perhaps you may discover a method of treatment that is more successful than one of those listed, or find a cure for a disease that no one has been able to treat before. If so, make the information known to others and you will be making a worthwhile contribution to the hobby.

Keeping a bit of the sea in your home can be an enjoyable experience. If your spark of enthusiasm for keeping marine fishes catches fire, pass on a few "glowing coals" to a friend.

William P. Braker.
Captiva Island, Florida.
June, 1966.

Hippocampus kuda—Yellow Seahorse.   A. VAN DEN NIEUWENHUIZEN

2   Establishing a salt-water tank

It is supposed that anyone venturing into the salt-water hobby has had previous experience keeping fresh-water fishes. If not, it would be better to backtrack and start with a fresh-water aquarium and fishes. Certain fundamentals apply to the successful management of both types of aquaria, but because both the equipment and the fish are less expensive for a fresh-water tank, it makes more sense to make the inevitable beginner's mistakes with the cheaper of the two. Better to lose fresh-water angelfish at 50c each than $5 salt-water angelfish.

Holocentrus xantherythrus—Squirrelfish.

Kinds of tanks: A tank to be used for a salt-water aquarium should be as corrosion-proof as possible. The ideal tank contains no metal, but tanks built solely from other materials have their disadvantages. Molded plexiglass tanks require a minimum of maintenance but they scratch easily and are not available in larger sizes. Molded fiberglass tanks are becoming more readily available and can be had in a variety of sizes and shapes, although they are expensive. The standard aquarium tank framed with salt-resistant steel or Monel Metal still seems to be the most practical and satisfactory.

Tank size is usually a matter of personal preference and a function of one's pocketbook, but a salt-water aquarium of less than 20 gallons is not practical. Salt-water fishes are more active and require more room than do fresh-water ones. Also, smaller tanks tend to foul much more readily. In general, the larger the tank, the more success you are likely to have with your marine aquarium.

The first thing to be done with any tank is to wash it out with a strong salt solution, avoiding soaps or detergents, followed by several flushes with clear water. This is usually sufficient to remove any toxic residue from the manu-facturing and assembly processes and from the tank sealant, although most name-brand cements are safe.

Location and lighting: After the tank has been selected and thoroughly cleaned, it is important to locate it properly. Salt-water tropical fishes are at least as sensitive to sudden temperature changes as their fresh-water counterparts, so care must be taken to place the tank away from any drafts or cold walls. Even though a heater is used, the failure of this piece of equipment could spell disaster if your tank is close to an outside wall or a window in the middle of winter. Likewise, to avoid overheating, the tank should not be placed near a radiator or other heat source. Light is also a consideration, and unless you want to be continually fighting algae choose a tank location that receives only a moderate amount of light. Because you will not need as much light for plant growth as you do with fresh-water tanks, it is necessary to illuminate just enough to highlight the tank and fishes.

Sand: The type of sand used on the bottom will be deter-mined in large part by the type of fish in the tank as well as by good tank-management practices. For example, the wrasses bury themselves at night, or when alarmed, so the sand must be loose enough to allow them to burrow. Hard-packed beach sand, therefore, is unsatisfactory. Very coarse, sharp sand or gravel might injure these fish in their burrowing attempts, and food and other organic matter may fall in between the particles, where it will decay and foul the tank. A good sand to use is the coral sand found on the beaches and sand flats of the Florida Keys and the Bahamas. If a little variety is wanted, the sand bottom can be alternated with coquina shells or coral rubble, but always keep in mind the burrowing fishes. If coral sand is not available, silica makes a good substitute. The grains should be about the size of a pinhead.

Sand should be thoroughly washed before it is put in the

tank. An easy way to do this is to put the sand in a bucket and introduce a garden hose with good pressure. The hose should be pushed all the way to the bottom of the bucket and moved around continuously until the water overflows clean and clear.

Put the sand in the aquarium so that it slopes slightly upwards from front to back. This will encourage dirt and uneaten food to work to the front of the tank where it can be siphoned off easily. The back is usually cluttered with rock and coral decorations, and having the sand shallower in front gives the tank a more natural appearance and eliminates the unsightly algae that often grow and decay on the inner

Rocks: Although a variety of rocks is available for decorating your tank, many of them are unsuitable, either for esthetic or practical reasons. For example, petrified wood is unnatural in a marine tank, and Ozark "coral", although interesting and attractive, dissolves and stains the water brown. There are many rocks that have a natural appearance and make excellent tank backgrounds. Some of these are coral rock, tufa, basalt, and Mexican lava. Tufa especially can be used to great advantage in constructing a natural-looking reef. It is a buff-colored volcanic rock, found in abundance around Sandusky, Ohio. Its surface is highly textured, full of small pits, cracks and tube-like formations, the latter caused by volcanic gases bubbling to the surface. This rock is quite likely to be full of dirt, and so will require quite a bit of soaking and hosing to clean it out. Being a comparatively soft rock, it is easy to work with hammer, chisel and screwdriver. If you happen to have a geologist's hammer, so much the better.

If you have several salt-water tanks and want an interesting contrast in one of them, use jet black basalt. This, too, is a volcanic rock but is extremely dense and hard, and difficult to work. It is impossible to shape the pieces, but as they have flat angular surfaces they can be fitted together to approximate horizontal, vertical or sloping strata.

Whether the rocks are laid together loosely or cemented together to make a more permanent exhibit will be a matter

A. VAN DEN NIEUWENHUIZEN

Gramma loreto—Royal Gramma.

of personal choice. It is difficult to put rocks together in such a way as to close all the spaces between them. Fish and other animals can hide and die in these holes, presenting a serious threat of contamination. If the holes are plugged with small bits of rock and cement, this problem will be eliminated. However, cementing the rocks together makes it more difficult to tear the tank down for cleaning. A solution is to cement a few rocks together which can then be lifted easily out of the tank, rather than to join all the decorations into one solid unit.

Interesting effects can be achieved by making overhanging ledges and creating small caves. It is sometimes necessary— and is more attractive—to have rocks projecting far beyond

Grammistes sexlineatus—Golden Stripe Grouper.

their balance point, but such rocks must be held or supported until the cement hardens. This is time-consuming and the smallest movement before the cement is set will break the joint. If a small amount of fast-setting hydraulic cement—such as Waterplug—is used to position the rock, much time and annoyance will be saved. The larger holes can be filled in later with ordinary cement.

Curing cement: Any tank in which cement has been used must be cured with a weak acid solution to neutralize the cement. Fill the tank with fresh water and add only enough acid (muriatic, acetic, or vinegar) to turn litmus paper red. The water should be tested daily and additional acid added if the litmus turns blue (becomes alkaline). When the water in the tank remains acidic for a few days, it is safe to siphon it off and flush the tank out with clean fresh water.

Shells and coral: After your tank is equipped with the necessary sand and rocks, you will want to consider some coral and shells to add to the decorations. If you live near the sea or vacation there, you can collect your own, otherwise they can be purchased from your dealer or from a shell collector.

Cleaning coral: Whatever the source, it is very important that all shells and coral be thoroughly cleaned and that the remains of the once living animals be removed. A very minute piece of flesh will of course not contaminate your tank, but many small pieces, such as the individual polyps in a coral head, will.

Any newly collected coral should be washed off as soon as possible with fresh water from a high-pressure garden hose. This will remove most of the slime and polyps. If a hose is not readily available, the coral should be kept immersed in water until it can be sprayed off.

Next it should be soaked in a strong chlorine solution to kill any remaining polyps and any burrowing shellfish or worms. Many household disinfectants, such as Clorox, consist primarily of chlorine in solution. Make sure that you do not use one containing a detergent as well. Such soaking is especially necessary for the large chunky corals like brain coral. After soaking in chlorine for several days, the coral should be rinsed several times in fresh water and allowed to bleach and dry in bright sunlight or under a sunlamp. Usually you will be able to determine whether or not all the chlorine has been washed out just by smelling. To make absolutely sure, place the coral in a small tank with a few superfluous guppies. If they survive, it is safe to put the coral in with your more expensive salt-water fish.

Preparing shells: Besides providing you with some attractive and decorative pieces, shell collecting can be an extremely interesting and rewarding hobby. Some collections by amateurs have been so good that they are now housed in public museums. Unless you can skin or scuba dive for your shells, you will pick up most of your specimens while walking the beaches, and they will most probably be empty. However, even these apparently clean shells should be carefully inspected and treated with chlorine like coral. If the shell has the odor of decay and the remains of the animal cannot be removed with a wire or thin knife, it should be buried in an ant hill for several weeks. The ants will do the rest. Placing the shell in a colony of mealworms will accomplish the same thing. To clean the outside of the shell, polish it with a fine wire brush mounted on an electric motor.

If you have collected a large shell with the live animal inside (a conch or helmet shell, for example) and want to remove the animal, boil it for five minutes and then pick out the animal with a knife or ice pick. Again, let the ants or mealworms finish the job.

Many small fishes use the shells in the aquarium as hiding-places. Gobies, blennies, cardinalfishes and damselfishes all make their homes in shells. As they defend their sanctuaries with considerable vigor, several shells should be provided in the tank or a considerable amount of fighting will take place.

Plants: It is almost impossible to grow or even keep plants in a marine aquarium. This is not to say that it cannot be done but it is so difficult and time-consuming that the average hobbyist is advised to forget about marine plants. There are some plastic grasses which are fairly good imitations of turtle and eel grass, and if a touch of green is wanted in the tank these may be used. There are also plastic sea fans which are reasonable facsimiles, and these come in different colors. Most authentic are the ones that are yellow and purple.

When the sand, rock, shells, coral, and other decorations have been chosen and arranged in the tank you are ready to add the water.

A. VAN DEN NIEUWENHUIZEN

Prionodes tigrinum—Harlequin Bass.

3 Sea water—natural or synthetic?

There are about as many opinions on the use of natural or artificial sea water as there are salt-water aquarists. Some swear by one, some the other, and still others prefer a mixture of the two. Opinions on circulation, filtration, and aeration also differ considerably, and each "expert" is convinced his method is the best. Actually a little common sense combined with sound basic aquarium management will result in a successful marine tank regardless of which type of water is used.

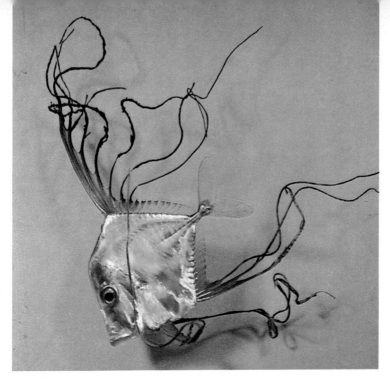

A. VAN DEN NIEUWENHUIZEN

Alectis crinitus—Threadfish.

Sea water: Those who have ready access to natural ocean water will probably want to use it, perhaps for economic reasons. To collect sea water, a spot should be chosen that is readily accessible, for there is no point in trudging blocks along a sandy beach or rocky shoreline carrying heavy buckets of water. If you have a boat at your disposal, so much the better as the water can then be collected away from the shore and any possible contamination. If it is not feasible to collect where the water is clear, you should plan to collect it well in advance of when it will be needed. This will allow time for the suspended material in the water to settle, and when it does the clear supernatant should be poured or

13

siphoned off into a clean container and this in turn allowed to settle again. If water is hard to come by, all of the dregs can be combined and, after these have settled for a sufficient length of time, the clear water salvaged. Some conservative aquarists claim that six weeks' storage in the dark is necessary.

Always use a non-toxic, non-corrosive container for collecting and storing sea water. Plastic buckets can be used to carry it from the beach to the car or truck where it can be poured into polyethylene bags, which are then sealed with a rubber band. This prevents the salt water from sloshing around your vehicle.

It is a good idea to have a reserve of water in readiness for an emergency. If your tank suddenly becomes polluted—and this can happen in a surprisingly short length of time—the best chance you have of saving your fish is to replace all, or almost all, of the water. This means you should always have on hand a volume of water equal to the volume of your display tank and at almost the same temperature, pH, and specific gravity. If you have several display tanks it is only necessary to have enough water to replace one of them, as it is unlikely that two or more tanks would become polluted at the same time.

If it is easy to replace the water, discard the contaminated tankful and drive to the beach for new; otherwise save the water and it will eventually clear itself. I once had some anemones, which I had collected at Shackleford Banks, North Carolina, in a gallon pickle jar. I attempted to keep them alive on the trip home, but on arriving all I had was a gallon of anemone chowder. Unable to approach within five feet of the jar I allowed it to stand and soon forgot about it. About a month later I rediscovered the jar and found the water to be crystal clear and completely free of odor. Of course, you do not want to wait a month for your water to clear, but within a week most of the bacterial action will have stopped and the water can be cleared with a power filter without clogging it too badly.

Artificial salt water: For the hobbyist who does not have a convenient source of natural sea water, there are several artificial sea water mixes available. Originally there were just one or two brands, but gradually the economic possibilities of the market were realized by more and more dealers until there are now about a dozen mixes available. It is impossible to test them all and evaluate their quality, but in general you cannot go wrong if one of the old established mixes is used. Several formulae are available if you wish to mix your own salts, but this is considerably more expensive than buying the prepared mixes. Many different compounds are required, some in minute quantities, and some of the latter are available commercially only in amounts that would last the average hobbyist years.

Regardless of what mix is used, follow the manufacturer's directions for preparing your salt water carefully. Be prepared, however, to wait for several days until a cloudiness, which no amount of filtration will remove, disappears. Again, you should be prepared to have an equal volume of artificial sea water in reserve for emergencies.

4 Keeping sea water in condition

Now that the tank has been filled with either natural or artificial salt water, steps must be taken to insure that the water remains in the good condition necessary for the successful maintenance of marine life.

Temperature: Probably the easiest factor to control is temperature. We are dealing here with *tropical* fish, and accordingly the temperature of the water should be about 78°F., as it is in the Bahamas and Florida Keys. Because aquarium fishes are in a relatively crowded situation and have less oxygen available, it is better to keep the temperature of the water between 72 to 74°F. At these temperatures water is capable of absorbing slightly more oxygen than at 78°F. Thermostats and heaters to control the temperatures are available in a variety of sizes and makes. Until quite recently only all-glass heaters and thermostats, which were easily broken, were available. They were also equipped with

Equetus acuminatus—Cubbyu.

metallic adjusting screws that became corroded. New models have a protective sleeve of perforated plastic round the glass tube to help protect it from shock, and the adjusting knobs and screws are all plastic.

During the summer, especially during prolonged hot spells, the temperature of your tank is quite likely to go above 80°F., with the result that the fish will become uncomfortable, and will huddle in corners or gasp at the surface for air. Moving the tank to a cooler room or the basement may help. Another solution is to run a coil of plastic hose through the tank leading from the cold water tap and back to the sink drain. A slow stream of cool water through the hose will help keep the temperature below 80°F.

A. VAN DEN NIEUWENHUIZEN

Equetus lanceolatus—Jackknife Fish (Juvenile).

As an emergency measure, ice cubes or block ice in a plastic bag can be floated in the tank. This has to be watched carefully as there is always the danger of cooling the tank too rapidly and too much.

Specific gravity: The next factor to consider is the specific gravity of the water, which goes hand in hand with salinity. A specific gravity of 1.025 is equivalent to 35 parts per thousand or 3.5% salt content. Most fishes can tolerate a wide range of specific gravity, but coral reef fishes are more accustomed to 1.025, so it is best for their well-being to keep the specific gravity at that reading. An inexpensive hydrometer costing only a few dollars is available at most stores dealing in salt-water fish. If you make up loss of water from evaporation with fresh water, the specific gravity of your saltwater will stay just about the same.

Pollution: Occasionally whole tanks of fish are lost because of pollution. The first indication of pollution is an increase in the respiratory rate of the fish and a general discomfort indicated by scratching, wild dashes and, eventually prostration. Pollution can be of two types: chemical or biological. Chemical pollution can be caused by toxic metals in contact with the water: paint fumes or insect sprays, a carelessly discarded cigar or cigarette, or soaps, detergents, or scouring powders that may have been used to clean the tank or aquarium equipment. An overdose of copper, used to discourage parasites, may also cause serious poisoning. Chemical pollution is difficult to correct, and as with most accidents, an ounce of prevention is worth a pound of cure. Once it occurs, the best course is to discard the water and replace it with your uncontaminated reserve. It is important to find the cause of the chemical contamination in order to prevent it in the future. A heavy aerator may be splashing water onto a light reflector with the drops running back into the tank. The metal frame of the tank may be exposed, or an over-zealous party guest may have fed his El Ropo to your favorite butterflyfish.

Biological pollution is almost always caused by over-feeding or by a dead fish or some other animal—starfish, snail or crab—that has been overlooked. The water takes on a characteristic milky-gray color and acquires an offensive odor. The color and the odor are caused by a bacterial bloom which, among other things, uses up the oxygen in the water. Carbon dioxide is also produced in large amounts. As a consequence, the fish are deprived of oxygen and, unless they belong to very hardy species, will die.

Most filters cannot operate fast enough, and indeed are not large enough, to remove such massive pollution. The most effective means of remedying the situation is to change the water completely and turn on strong aeration, in addition to operating the filter at full capacity. If another tank is available and it is practical to move some fish into it, do so.

Filters: In order to maintain maximum water clarity and reduce contamination in the tank, a good high-capacity filter should be used. It is not possible to overfilter your tank but marine aquaria are frequently underfiltered. The minimum filtering rate should be a complete turnover once every four hours, but this will give you no margin for an emergency. If you can provide a filter or filters that will turn over the tank every two hours, so much the better, and once an hour is ideal. A filter of this capacity provides a bonus in that it not only clears up the water faster but because of the high turnover rate will produce a current in the tank that many coral reef fishes enjoy. Filters of this size are usually operated by a small electric pump rather than by an air lift.

The effectiveness of a filter is dependent on the particle size, rate of flow, and filter area. An ideal rate of flow is one gallon per square foot per minute, but because a filter of this size is impractical for most home aquaria, the flow rate should be figured at twice this amount, or two gallons per square foot per minute. This means, for example, that a 60-gallon tank being filtered at the maximum turnover rate of once an hour should be equipped with a filter or filters with a total surface area of 72 square inches. This may seem like a large filter to someone who has had experience only in keeping fresh-water fishes, but you will find that your salt-water charges will be considerably more healthy and active when given the benefit of a large filter and fast turnover rate.

The exact make and type of filter will ultimately be the choice of the owner, but it is recommended that outside box-type filters rather than inside or sub-sand filters be used, because of the ease of cleaning and faster turnover rate. Air lift filters of the high-lift type and power filters should be used to give sufficient turnover, and an extra power filter may be kept in readiness to clean up a stubborn tank or to help out if a tank becomes fouled.

The filtering material should be built up in layers, graduated in size. The bottom layer should be rather coarse sand or fine gravel, roughly $\frac{1}{8}''$ to $\frac{3}{16}''$ diameter. This first layer should be limestone, crushed shell, or coral sand and rubble. It will do no mechanical filtering but it will help to maintain the proper pH, keeping the water on the alkaline

Centropyge argi—Cherubfish.

side, and it also supports the upper layers of finer sand and prevents them from passing through the filter. On top of this buffering layer should be placed successively finer layers of coral, quartz, silica or flint sand, activated carbon or charcoal, and finally spun nylon or nylon felt on top. This last is much better than glass wool as it can be washed out under a faucet and used again, and it does not break up and penetrate your fingers. The charcoal should be neither too large nor too small. Large pieces do not provide enough absorptive area, and very fine charcoal is apt to be too dusty. The ideal size is somewhere between a rice grain and half a pea. Before putting the charcoal into the filter it should be boiled in clean water in order to drive out all the air. If the

Centropyge flavissimus—Lemonpeel.

charcoal is put in the filter without doing this, it will not function at peak efficiency.

Several filter aids have been developed for salt-water tanks. These aids combine an activated carbon and an ion-exchange resin in pre-packaged units. In addition to providing sparkling clear water, they help maintain pH and remove certain toxic metallic ions from the water. The only drawback to using these filter aids is their cost.

Many aquarists object to algae in their filters. Actually the algae are not harmful but, on the contrary, beneficial. Today many large public aquaria are building supplementary filters where algae are encouraged to grow, the excess being regularly removed. These plants improve the quality of the water by removing harmful nitrogenous wastes from the water, and utilizing them in their own metabolic processes. They also contribute a small but still measurable amount of oxygen and take up some of the carbon dioxide given off by the fishes. More will be said about this under Aeration.

Aeration: It may be necessary to provide aeration for your tank, even if you have good filtration and circulation. If you have crowded your tank or the water temperature is high, an aerator must be put into the tank. The aerator itself adds some oxygen to the water but it also serves to circulate the water within the tank, bringing oxygen-deficient water to the surface and oxygen-laden water to the bottom. A good deal of the vital carbon dioxide exchange takes place at the surface, and in a crowded or overheated tank it is necessary to speed up this process as much as possible.

Important as it is to have sufficient oxygen in the water, it is equally important to remove the carbon dioxide. Even though oxygen may be at the saturation level, fish may still suffocate if the carbon dioxide level is high. An excess of carbon dioxide in the water interferes with the uptake of oxygen by the blood. By far the best way to eliminate carbon dioxide is by strong aeration. While plants (algae) produce oxygen and utilize carbon dioxide, the extent to which they do so, as compared to the gas exchange that takes place at the surface, is usually small.

pH: If your tank is properly filtered, aerated, and is free from pollution, the pH of the water will not change appreciably. pH is a measure of alkalinity or acidity, and is a number that represents the hydrogen-ion concentration in a solution. It is expressed by a scale of 0–14, with the mid-point 7 being neutral. Anything below 7 is considered acidic and above that point basic or alkaline. The normal pH of seawater is 8.3, which is definitely basic. Although fishes can tolerate slight changes in pH, it should not be allowed to go below 8.0. The pH of your water can be checked periodically with an inexpensive kit made especially for testing sea water. Kits manufactured for fresh water will not give the proper reading of sea water.

If the pH has slipped below 8.0, there may be several causes. The first thing to check is the aeration. An excess of carbon dioxide (CO_2) will cause an acid condition. Another cause may be a clogged or non-functioning filter which is not removing waste products from the tank. The buffering layer of coral or limestone chips should be cleaned and more material added when necessary. Adding small amounts of sodium bicarbonate (baking soda) occasionally, via the filter, will help keep the pH at a normal level.

5 Feeding

What has been written, said, and learned about good feeding practices for fresh-water fishes applies to salt-water specimens—but in spades. It is extremely important not to overfeed because this is one of the major causes of pollution. Many salt-water fish are fussy eaters and they must be coaxed to accept the strange foods they are offered in captivity. If one food is refused, try another and still another until they start to eat. Perhaps the trouble is not in the food itself but the form in which it is offered. Some species prefer chunks of food, some like strips or small cubes, and others want their food ground or mashed. When all else fails, live food should be offered. It takes a pretty strong fish constitution to ignore live adult brine shrimp! Of course, this is the ideal food but it is not available in all parts of the country. Even where it is available, shipments are quite often irregular as a result of poor hatches in the brine ponds or for other reasons.

Feeding schedule: Anyone who has spent some time watching fish with mask, snorkle, and flippers must be impressed with the fact that many small fishes spend a good part of their time searching for food. Eating is a continual process that goes on from the time the fish comes out of its sand burrow or shell retreat in the morning until darkness sends it back home each night. This should give fish keepers a clue as to how to feed their charges. Small portions fed

Pomacanthus annularis—Blue Ring Angelfish.

frequently may become wearing for the aquarist but are best for the fish. There are exceptions to this, of course, but the majority of small marine fishes will respond positively to frequent feedings.

Establish a time schedule when it is convenient for you to feed, and then stick to that routine. If it is possible to feed three times a day, do so. A good schedule would be before or after breakfast, late afternoon or early evening, and a little before turning out the tank light for the night, allowing enough time for the fish to consume everything before you do so since most fish will not eat in the dark. Again it is important to remember not to feed too much. Offer your fish only what they can easily consume in five minutes. If any food remains after five minutes, you have given them too much. Needless to say, any uneaten food should be removed immediately.

Pomacanthus arcuatus—French Angelfish.

Change of menu: Just as you would tire of eating the same thing day after day (even though it were filet mignon), so do the fish in your tank. You have a choice, however. You can either get a new cook or go to another restaurant. Your fish have no choice. They must eat what you offer them or starve, and many do just that. Tired of the same fare, they will slow down or stop eating altogether and eventually die of starvation. Those that continue to eat, if not getting a balanced diet, may wither away from malnutrition.

There is a surprising variety of foods that you can obtain from the butcher shop, grocer's shelves, fish market, or local pet store. Many fish will relish small strips or cubes of lean beef steak or beef heart. All the fat should be trimmed from any meat fed to your fish. Pork should be avoided altogether. Several kinds of seafood can be fed, including smelt, halibut and snapper. Oily fishes such as herring and blue runner may be offered occasionally but not regularly as the oil has a tendency to clog the tank-filter and reduce its efficiency. Shrimp, crabmeat, and other shellfish, such as clams and scallops, are excellent. Of course, you should always have a supply of frozen shrimp to offer your fish, and this can be fed continuously along with the other items. Some fish will prefer Tubifex, others Chironomus (bloodworms), while still others will do nicely on dry or paste food.

Live food: There are species that will refuse everything except live food. Among them are sargassumfish, cardinalfish, and most seahorses. These should be given live brine shrimp or young guppies of suitable size. The sargassumfish is cannibalistic and should not be kept with other smaller sargassumfish or, for that matter, any smaller fish that it is capable of engulfing in its capacious maw.

Hatching brine shrimp: For young or very small fishes there is nothing better than newly-hatched brine shrimp. Hatching brine shrimp eggs is very simple, and you can be assured of a constant supply of live food for your small fry if you have several hatching jars operating at the same time. For small quantities of shrimp, quart jars are large enough. If you have quite a number of fish to feed, gallon jars should be used. To every gallon of fresh water add one-half cup of salt and a teaspoonful of borax. Mix and dissolve thoroughly and introduce an air stone that gives a strong current of air, so that the water "boils". Add about one teaspoonful of brine shrimp eggs and allow 24 to 48 hours for hatching.

To remove the hatched shrimp, cut off the air supply and let the jar stand undisturbed for half an hour or until the egg cases and shrimp larvae have separated. The pink shrimp will settle to the bottom while the brown egg cases will float to the top of the jar. Carefully insert a rubber or plastic hose to the bottom of the jar and siphon off the shrimp, straining them out with a fine-mesh cloth, (a handkerchief will do), and collecting the salt water in a plastic or glass container. The water can be re-used several times.

It is important that the shrimp be separated from the egg cases. Small fishes, especially baby seahorses, cannot digest the shells and their digestive systems become impacted with them.

If all the shrimp are not consumed at one feeding they can be saved until the next, or even for several days, by keeping them in salt water in the refrigerator. I have kept adult shrimp this way for ten days.

Three basic rules: In summary, there are three basic rules of feeding: feed sparingly but often; change both the kind and shape of food; be patient with fussy eaters.

6 Fish diseases

There are a few fish diseases that can be recognized without sophisticated laboratory equipment, but most require scientifically trained personnel and a battery of microscopes, staining equipment, glassware, and even electronic equipment. Certain diseases and disorders such as internal tumors, functional disorders, and organ degeneration are incurable and it is best to destroy the fish rather than throw good money after bad trying to cure it.

Preventive measures: Most fishes purchased from reputable dealers will be in a healthy condition when you get them, but it is still best to isolate new additions for a few days to make sure they are not carrying some disease or parasite still in the incubation period. In addition, your new fish should be given a sterilizing dip in potassium permanganate solution, 25 mg. (roughly 1/3 grain) per gallon for about two minutes. If the fish show signs of distress before the time is up, they can be removed and the dip repeated after an hour or so. While the fish are in their isolation tank they can also be given a treatment with copper sulfate in order to make relatively sure they are carrying no external parasites. Concentrations for the copper treatment are given below.

One of the most devastating diseases in an aquarium is an

A. VAN DEN NIEUWENHUIZEN

Holacanthus tricolor—Rock Beauty.

epidemic of **Oodinium**. This is a protozoan related to the organisms that cause the red tides. (Oodinium infection in fresh-water fishes is known as Velvet.) In its first stages it is invisible to the naked eye but as it multiplies and grows larger, the fish becomes covered with small white dots. If not treated they may become so numerous that the whole fish

Chelmon rostratus—Copperband Butterflyfish.

Chaetodon capistratus—Four Eye Butterflyfish.

appears white. At first the organism attacks the gills and interferes with respiration; it is usually at this point that the aquarist realizes that something is wrong. The fish huddle in a corner or make frantic dashes around the tank as if trying to shake loose or rub off the irritation.

The best and cheapest treatment for this parasite is copper

sulfate, but as this is toxic to fish it must be used with great caution. A concentration of 0.15 parts per million (ppm) is sufficient to rid the fish and the tank of parasites in a week to ten days. To obtain this concentration make a stock solution of copper sulfate by dissolving one gram in a pint (16 fl. oz.) of distilled water. Use one cc (20 drops) of this stock solution for each gallon of salt water, remembering to take into consideration the water that has been displaced by rocks, coral and other tank decorations. If this is not done, the concentration of copper may be too great and you will kill some of your more delicate specimens. Most crabs and lobsters can take this concentration of copper, but other invertebrates, such as sea anemones, live corals, and starfish, should be removed and kept in a separate tank during treatment. It will not be necessary to change the water after the fish are cured for the copper will gradually disappear as it combines with the coral and carol sand to form an insoluble compound: copper carbonate.

Another external parasite that can be cured by the use of copper is a small fluke, **Benedenia**, formerly known as Epibdella. Again the fish are seen to scratch themselves and huddle with fins folded. The eyes are usually the most severely affected part, and if not treated they become clouded over and eventually swell up and burst. Years ago the treatment for this disease was to dip the fish in fresh water for several minutes or until the parasite was killed. This frequently was as damaging to the fish as it was to the parasite.

Fishes may often be seen huddling, scratching, and going through the same signs of distress that were described above. There is no fin erosion, however, no eye irritation and apparently no gill damage. Microscopic examination usually reveals a small ciliate which as yet has not been identified. It can be eliminated, however, by dipping the fish in a 1 : 1000 solution of acetic acid (1 teaspoon to approx. $4\frac{1}{2}$ gallons) for one minute, or longer if the fish can take the treatment. Several dips may be necessary. Damselfishes particularly seem to be affected by this organism.

For many years seahorses have been collected and shipped while heavily infested with the copepod **Arqulus**. Up until now the only way to rid the seahorses of this parasite was to pick each one off separately with tweezers. Just recently, however, Warren Zeiller of the Miami Seaquarium has made some tests on a new product, anthium dioxide, and found it very effective in eliminating these pests. It is basically a chlorine compound and is to be marketed under the name of Microcide. This product should be used in an isolation tank at a concentration of 0.2 ppm (parts per million, parts of water, by weight). After 48 hours the seahorses will be free from Arqulus and can be put into your display tank.

Fin rot, tail rot, and various body lesions can be treated in several ways. If the fish is easy to catch, it should be removed from the tank and the affected area swabbed or painted with a good antiseptic solution. The fish should then be kept in a reserve tank for observation. Several solutions can be used, among them potassium permanganate, merthiolate, mercurochrome, and the product known as ST-37. If several fishes, or a whole tank, are infected by the same type of bacterial disease, treatment can be carried on right in the tank. A combination of penicillin, chloromycetin, and streptomycin (250 mg. of each for every three gallons of water) is usually effective against almost all bacterial infections. It is usually not necessary to repeat the treatment nor to change the water after treatment.

Occasionally a creamy white, bumpy growth will appear on the fins and body of various fishes. This is **Lymphocystis**, a virus disease. No cure is known but it is not always fatal. About half the time the lesions will disappear and the fish will recover. As the disease seems to be contagious it is best to remove any affected fishes and isolate them until they either recover or die.

Popeye, a condition in which the eye bulges or sticks out far beyond its normal position, may be caused by any one or more of several things. Occasionally water may become supersaturated with air, due to a pinhole on the suction line of a pump or power filter. This air is taken up by the fishes before it can escape to the atmosphere. As it passes through fine capillaries such as those in the eye, the air expands, rupturing the capillaries, and escapes into the eye proper, causing it to bulge. Bacterial infection may also cause

Chaetodon lunula—Orange Butterflyfish.

Heniochus acuminatus—Bannerfish.

Dascyllus aruanus—Black and White Dascyllus.

popeye, and sometimes the fish will respond to treatment with sulfathiazole (one-half teaspoon to the gallon) in its tank, or a pinch added to its food. Swabbing the eye with argyrol solution, 5%, may also help.

7 Popular salt-water fishes

Yellow Seahorse—*Hippocampus kuda* (Family: *Syngnathidae*). One of the favorite fish of visitors to a public aquarium is the seahorse. People are captivated by its appearance and its habit of clinging to coral, seawhips and other seahorses with its prehensile tail. The seahorse's strange reproductive behavior is also fascinating. In this group of fishes, the female deposits her eggs in the brood pouch of the male, who incubates them for a period of eight to ten days depending on the water temperature and the species. The young are expelled from the pouch with considerable force, owing to the contortions of the male trying to relieve himself of this burden. The young of the Atlantic spotted seahorse (*Hippocampus erectus*) are about $\frac{5}{8}''$ at "birth". According to Earl S. Herald, Director of the Steinhart Aquarium, they reach their maximum size of five inches in about ten months.

Seahorses are among the most difficult aquarium fishes to feed and raise. They usually require live food, and the young must be provided with newly hatched brine shrimp on an almost round-the-clock basis. Brine shrimp hatched and separated as described earlier in this book will satisfy the young for a week or two, after which they require slightly larger food. The shrimp themselves will have to be grown by being fed on a mixture of yeast and green water. Half-grown to adult seahorses can eat live adult brine shrimp, or *Gammarus* if these are available.

Seahorses should be provided with the dried and cleaned skeleton of a seawhip or thin piece of drift wood to use as a hitching post. There are more than two dozen species of seahorses found all over the world in tropical and temperate marine waters. They range in size from $1\frac{1}{2}$ to 12 inches.

Squirrelfish—*Holocentrus xantherythrus* (*Holocentridae*). A squirrelfish will add a touch of red to a marine tank. These fish, however, are largely nocturnal and prefer to hide away during the day. Usually they can be seen lurking in a hole in the rocks or under a ledge, from where they dash out to grab a meal. They are not fussy eaters; they will grab almost anything that is offered to them. Their large mouths enable them to take a fairly large chunk of cut fish or shrimp, so they ignore very small food. For this reason it is best not to keep them with smaller fishes or they will make a meal of some of your favorite specimens.

On a collecting trip to Bimini in the Bahamas one year, we had trouble with adult male bluehead wrasses. Each day several more would be thrown into the holding box but their numbers never increased. The cage was inspected underwater from the outside with scuba gear, but we found no possible escape route. On the day that the box was finally emptied of all its fishes the cause of the disappearances was found. Two longspine squirrelfish had accidentally got into the bluehead holding cage and had become quite fat at their, and our, expense. The less attractive "slippery dicks" had been ignored.

Care should be taken when handling squirrelfish. They are quite spiny and a wound from either the dorsal spines or the preopercular spine can be quite painful. I once dropped one of these fellows on my foot. The cheek spine penetrated my sneakers and entered my small toe down to the bone. It was several weeks before I could walk without a limp.

Many species are offered for sale but the smaller ones, such as *Holocentrus vexillarius* from Florida and the Bahamas and *H. diadema* from the Pacific, are more desirable for home tanks. There are about 70 species distributed around the world in tropical waters.

Royal Gramma—*Gramma loreto* (*Serranidae*). One of the most attractive fishes to come to the salt-water hobby is the royal gramma. This attractive little fish is one of the groupers or sea basses. Because of its habit of hanging upside-down under rock ledges it was overlooked for a long time by divers and collectors, and then it was found only in water at a depth

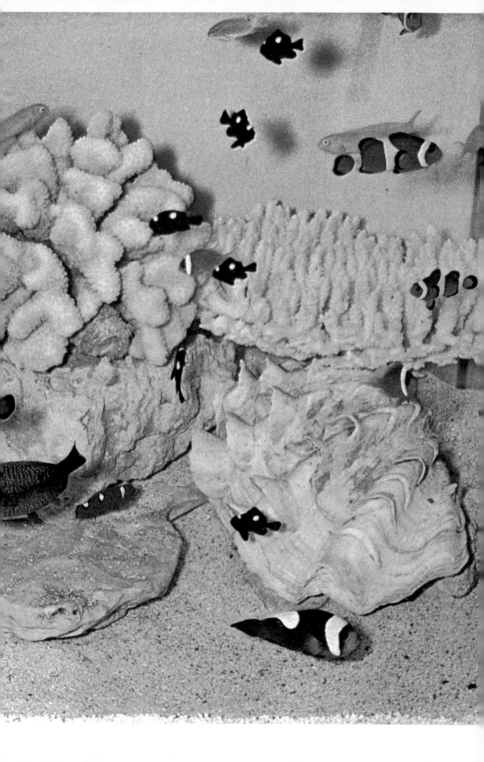

of 40 or 50 feet. Fish brought up from this depth have a difficult time adjusting to the difference in pressure and many were killed until techniques were worked out for bringing them to the surface gradually. Naturally the time and effort required to bring these fish in alive made them quite expensive. Lately it has been found that in some localities *Gramma* is found in water as shallow as 10 or 15 feet, which should eliminate most of the problems of collecting them.

The royal gramma is not a very active fish. It spends a considerable amount of time hanging quietly under a rock or coral. When it does move it does so in short spurts, resting in between dashes in a head up, tail down sloping position.

Live food is best for this species. It will eat adult brine shrimp with relish and should be given an occasional live guppy of appropriate size, along with some chopped clam.

One of the smallest of a family, some members of which reach 1,000 pounds, the gramma grows to four inches. It is found throughout the West Indies.

Golden Stripe Grouper—*Grammistes sexlineatus* (*Serranidae*). This old favorite has been imported for years. It is a striking fish showing golden yellow stripes and dashes against a black background. Younger fishes have the lines on the side made up of a series of short dashes, but as the fish grows older and increases in size the dashes join end to end to form longer streaks. Like most groupers *Grammistes* has a large mouth and a voracious appetite. It will eat anything that does not eat it first, so care must be taken to put it with fishes of equal and larger size. It is not fussy about its food and will do well if offered a variety of cut fish, raw shrimp and perhaps an occasional live goldfish, large guppy or molly. Given proper care it can be expected to grow to ten inches and live for years in captivity.

This is a widely distributed Indo-Pacific species of a large family, the members of which are found all around the world in tropical and temperate waters.

Harlequin Bass—*Prionodes tigrinum* (*Serranidae*). *Prionodes* is a peaceful little fish that seems to respect the adage "Live and let live". Once it is established in your tank you will hardly notice it except at feeding time, when it will come out like a well-mannered and well-trained dog to accept its share of the meal. Usually you will have to look closely to find this fish as it blends in so well with almost any type of background. Except at feeding time, the harlequin bass is found resting quietly on the bottom or perched on a rock, propped up slightly on its fins.

This is not a particularly abundant species, and it is not easily spotted underwater by collectors. This is probably one of the reasons why it is not offered for sale more frequently.

Live and frozen brine shrimp, very small guppies, and diced clams or scallops should be fed. Its most common size is three to four inches.

Threadfish—*Alectis crinitus* (*Carangidae*). The threadfish, which until recently was known as *Alectis ciliaris*, is the juvenile form of a large jack known as the African pompano. For years they had been considered separate species until, through a study of a series of these fishes, ichthyologists were able to determine that they were one and the same.

The jacks in general do not make good aquarium fishes as they are active swimmers and need plenty of room to move around. The threadfish is the exception to the rule. It is a relatively quiet species, usually moving slowly but steadily around the tank.

The most striking feature of this fish is the extremely long trailing streamers of the dorsal and anal fin rays, which are about twice as long as the fish itself. As the fish grows the streamers become shorter and eventually shrink to a more normal length. Except for the fins, which have a pale yellow coloration, the fish is all silver with about five faint dark bars on the sides.

Although this fish is found in inshore waters it is not a typical coral reef fish. When it becomes an adult it moves out to open water and enjoys quite a reputation as a sport fish. The threadfish should be given as large a tank as possible and one that is not cluttered with decorations.

Like all jacks, this species prefers live food. If it will not readily accept the dry or cut food you offer, tempt it with live adult brine shrimp or a few small guppies. Usually they

Dascyllus trimaculatus—Three Spot Dascyllus.

can be weaned away from this more expensive food but it takes a bit of patience. Fishes about three inches long make good aquarium specimens.

Many of the more than 200 species in this family are excellent food fishes, especially the pompanos.

Cubbyu—*Equetus acuminatus* (*Sciaenidae*). The *Equetus* group is the most spectacular of the drum family. With the exception of the spotted seatrouts, most members of this family are rather drab fishes.

A. VAN DEN NIEUWENHUIZEN

Amphiprion percula—Clown Anemonefish.

The cubbyu is a rather delicate little fish and requires special handling. It is a weak swimmer and is usually found near the bottom. It appears to be nocturnal as it is found under loose rocks during the day and around piers and pilings at night. Usually three or four will be found together, feeding in the same small area or under the same rock.

As this fish feeds on the bottom it should be offered the type of food that it is apt to find there: small crabs, shrimps and other crustaceans, marine worms, and very small shellfish. Now unless you happen to live next door to the sea and can shake these things out of seaweed you will have to substitute as best you can. In place of small crabs feed a little finely-cut crab meat or lobster tail, which can be saved next time you have either of these for your own dinner. In place of marine worms, bloodworms (*Chironomus*) can be fed (although these are, of course, insect larvae, not worms), while finely-diced clam, scallop, oyster or freshwater mussel will do for shellfish.

In spite of the fact that these fish do not enjoy being handled, they live quite well in a tank once they are established. Do everything you can, however, to avoid moving or transferring them any more often than necessary. A tank at the John G. Shedd Aquarium containing several dozen of these fish had to be emptied and the fish moved after they had been established for six months or more. They were put into a tank of equal size with the same water system, but more than half of them died, even though the handling was done very carefully.

The cubbyu grows to a length of about eight inches, but four- to five-inch fish are most satisfactory for the home aquarium.

Jacknife Fish—*Equetus lanceolatus* (*Sciaenidae*). The jacknife is a particularly handsome species which immediately catches the eye with its long tapering first dorsal fin. This fish is slightly larger than the cubbyu but its habits and requirements are practically the same.

Even though these fish and the preceding species are weak swimmers, they can put on surprising bursts of speed of short duration which are generally sufficient to carry them to the other side of a rock or coral head, out of range of the collecting net.

A third species, the spotted drum, a much rarer form from deeper water, is seldom seen either in public or home aquaria.

The jacknife fish is usually seen about six inches long, but can grow to perhaps ten inches.

Cherubfish—*Centropyge argi* (*Chaetodontidae*). Known for a long time as the pigmy angelfish, the name "cherubfish" has been applied and accepted by the Committee on Common

Names of the American Fisheries Society and the American Society of Ichthyologists and Herpetologists. A big introduction for a small fish!

This is another specimen from deep water. It is not very difficult to capture but it must be brought up with care from depths of 50 to 60 feet.

This fish must be given plenty of hiding places in an aquarium. It seems to live much better and is more active if it has plenty of rocks behind which to hide. It is a fighting fish and several in a tank will constantly chase each other, the dominant one driving the others into submission if sufficient refuges are not provided. Towards other species it is rather peaceful and disputes over territory do not usually occur.

It does well on a diet of frozen and live adult brine shrimp and seems to enjoy nibbling on a rock covered with algae.

It grows to a length of three inches, and is native to the tropical Atlantic region.

Lemonpeel—*Centropyge flavissimus* (*Chaetodontidae*). This is probably one of the prettiest little fishes to come to the attention of marine aquarists in a long time. It is completely yellow except for touches of blue around the eye, the gill cover and on the fins. Hence its name "lemonpeel" is quite apt.

It is not as territorial as the preceding species, but is quite a peaceful fish and manages to go its own way in the aquarium without disrupting the status quo.

Another species, the bicolor cherubfish, is more like the lemonpeel in temperament, but closer in size to the Atlantic cherubfish. It is suggestive of the color pattern of the Atlantic rock beauty, yellow on the forward part of the body and dark on the back half, with a yellow tail. In fact, it has often been called the Pacific rock beauty.

As with the cherubfish, both of these species will readily accept adult brine shrimp, and will sometimes enjoy a treat of minced shellfish.

Both the lemonpeel and the bicolor cherubfish are Pacific species belonging to a family that contains more than 150 species. Most are shallow water marine fishes, although some do go into brackish water.

Amphiprion akallopisos—Pink Skunk Anemonefish.

Blue Ring Angelfish—*Pomacanthus annularis* (*Chaetodontidae*). As with many other members of this family, the blue ring angelfish changes considerably in color and pattern as it matures. The juvenile is hardly recognizable as the same fish after it reaches adulthood. This is further complicated by the fact that the young of many of these Pacific angelfish are quite similar. For this reason different species have been classified as the same fish, and different stages of the same fish have been described as separate species. The young of this fish, the Koran, and the imperial angelfish are all dark blue, with lighter blue or white lines which form backward-curving, semi-circular markings on the sides of the body. The blue ring angelfish gets its name from the almost perfect blue ring located behind the eye and above the gill opening in the adult fish.

Amphiprion laticlavius—Saddleback Anemonefish.

These fish are usually imported as adults or half-grown fish measuring six to eight inches. They require a larger tank than do most of the other species described here, and should have one of at least 50 gallons.

They like ground food but will take small pieces of cut fish, shrimp or clam.

The blue ring angelfish is native to the central Indo-Pacific area.

French Angelfish—*Pomacanthus arcuatus* (*Chaetodontidae*). The French angelfish is one of the most popular and readily obtainable marine fishes. It has been offered on dealers' price-lists almost since the inception of the hobby and continues to remain a favorite.

The young of this species are black, with prominent

yellow bars. As the fish grows older the scales acquire a yellow edge, and the yellow bars are retained but become more diffuse. Young black angels are quite similar to young French angels, and it takes an experienced eye to see the differences. This can be done, however, by observing the mouth and tail. In the black angelfish, the yellow band on the upper lip is interrupted by two black marks, while in the French this band is continuous. Also, the posterior portion of the caudal fin of the black is quite pale, while the whole fin of the French angelfish is black and edged with yellow.

Both the French and the black angelfish adjust well to aquarium conditions. They seem to prefer soft food such as ground raw shrimp, and to this can be added a bit of raw spinach or kale.

Care must be taken when mixing specimens of different sizes. In the confines of a tank a three-inch fish will chase and kill one that is smaller, unless the tank has sufficient hiding-places. This is not the case, however, when there is a great discrepancy in size.

The French angelfish is found on both sides of the tropical Atlantic, whereas the black is native only to the Americas.

Rock Beauty—*Holocanthus tricolor* (*Chaetodontidae*). The rock beauty is another of those fishes that changes color and pattern with growth. When it is very young, about an inch long, it is solid orange, except for a black spot ringed with blue on the upper sides just in front of the tail. As the fish grows, the black spot increases in size until in the adult fish it covers slightly more than the rear half.

This is another species that must be carefully selected as to size if two or more are to be kept together. The larger of the two will constantly chase the smaller, except, of course, if the difference in size is very great. Rock beauties pick on other fishes if they have the slightest mark or injury showing. A fish with a bad eye will be chased and tormented until the eye has been picked out. So although rock beauties are very desirable from a standpoint of beauty and hardiness, they have to be watched very closely to prevent them from injuring your other fishes.

On the coral reef this fish can be seen constantly feeding.

It spends a good part of its time browsing algae and picking small invertebrates from rocks. It should be fed both live and frozen adult brine shrimp and occasionally some lettuce, spinach or kale to supplement its diet.

The best rock beauty for the home aquarium is about three inches long, but if you have a tank of sixty gallons or more, a six-inch fish would not be too large.

It grows to a length of eight to ten inches and is found in the American tropical Atlantic, from Florida to Rio de Janeiro.

Copperband Butterfly—*Chelmon rostratus* (*Chaetodontidae*). To the best of my knowledge this fish has no common name except longnose butterflyfish. This is confusing, as there is another butterflyfish, *Forcipiger longirostris*, from the same general area with an equally long nose, and it also, strangely enough, is called the longnose butterflyfish. I am proposing, therefore, that this fish be known as the copperband butterflyfish, with the hope that the name will come into general usage.

According to Earl S. Herald in "Living Fishes of the World", the copperband was thought for quite some time to be the archerfish, because a specimen of *Chelmon* accompanied the original description of the spitting habits of *Toxotes*. It was not until 1926, 162 years later, that the confusion was cleared up by Dr George S. Myers and Dr Hugh M. Smith, who described the mechanism by which the archerfish expels its watery bullets.

Perhaps the most striking feature of this fish is the long tubular mouth which it uses to great advantage in obtaining its food. This "beak" is of particular advantage in poking into small holes and cracks to pick out the small organisms hiding there. In this it definitely has the advantage over many other fishes.

Because of its small mouth the copperband butterfly must have small food. Adult brine shrimp are about the largest food it can eat, and even these should be sifted and strained so that the smaller sizes can be fed. *Tubifex* can be alternated with the shrimp.

This fish is found throughout the eastern and central Indo-Pacific, where it grows to a length of about five inches.

A. VAN DEN NIEUWENHUIZEN
Microspathodon chrysurus—Yellowtail Damselfish.

Four Eye Butterflyfish—*Chaetodon capistratus* (*Chaetontidae*). What is said here about the care and feeding of the Foureye butterfly can apply equally as well, with some few exceptions, to the entire group of butterfly fishes. Although butterflies and angelfishes are in the same family, the angelfishes are generally larger and their requirements differ accordingly. The two groups differ on the basis of the presence or absence of a strong spine on the lower margin of the preoperculum. It is present in the angelfish group.

The foureye is a very satisfactory aquarium fish. It is peaceful, feeds well, is fairly hardy in captivity and does not seem to be bothered by other fishes. The false eye on the side of the fish, which is found in many other species, is apparently a bit of disguise to confuse predators about which is the head and which is the tail end of the fish.

In nature, foureyes are usually found in pairs. It is almost axiomatic that where one is found, another will be close by.

Coris gaimardi—Yellowtail Wrasse (Young).

More often than not two are taken in a trap. While diving, a pair will be found around a coral head, an old anchor, or a pile of shells. If one of the pair is netted, the other is quite reluctant to leave the area.

In the aquarium these fish do not need much room, but of course the more you can give them the better. They have small mouths and require either ground or finely-chopped food, brine shrimp or *Chironomus* larvae.

The foureye is a small butterfly, averaging about three inches, and is found in the West Indies and Florida. Some Pacific members of this family, such as *Chaetodon lineolatus*, reach a foot in length.

Orange Butterflyfish—*Chaetodon lunula (Chaetodontidae)*. This is a common species in and around Hawaii. It exhibits a considerable change in color pattern as it grows. The young show none of the raccoon-like mask that is present in the adult.

The orange butterfly is one of the hardiest of this family in captivity and it is easy to obtain. It should be fed as described under other butterflyfish species.

It grows to a length of six inches, and is found from the Red Sea to Hawaii.

Bannerfish—*Heniochus acuminatus* (*Chaetontidae*). Along with the Moorish idol, the bannerfish has probably been pictured and illustrated more than any other fish. Although it is one of the butterflyfish, it differs from most of them in the fact that it has a much deeper body, due to its highly arched back. The other outstanding feature is the length of the fourth dorsal spine which may be several inches long and from which the fish gets its common name.

As attractive as this fish is, it is unfortunate that it is not more hardy in captivity. Occasional specimens will become adapted to tank life, but the majority of them do not do well. It takes an experienced aquarist and one with a lot of patience to encourage these fish to adjust to captivity. They must be handled with the utmost care, and should not be startled in any way.

Heniochus is a fussy eater and it will have to be offered a variety of foods before it will eat. Water quality must be the best. Any open wounds it receives should be treated immediately. This fish is not recommended for the beginner. It is native to the Indo-Pacific, and grows to a length of eight inches.

Black and White Dascyllus—*Dascyllus aruanus* (*Pomacentridae*). This family supplies many of the fishes kept both in home and in public aquaria. The reason for their popularity is their hardiness and adaptability to captivity. Included in this group, with others, are fishes of the genera *Dascyllus*, *Amphiprion*, *Chromis*, *Eupomacentrus*, and *Abudefduf*.

The *Dascyllus* group has a habit of congregating around coral heads, hovering above the fingers of the coral like a swarm of bees. When a larger fish or skin diver approaches they disappear into the holes in the coral, almost in unison. If the piece of coral is small enough the collector can pick it up with the fish still inside.

Dascyllus aruanus has been imported for many years and continues to be a favorite. Quite often it is confused with *D. melanurus*, which has a black tail instead of the clear tail of *D. Aruanus*.

These little fish will eat almost anything that is offered to them. They should be fed small portions frequently, and all food left on the bottom should be removed. They seem to be more at ease if given coral or rocks to hide among.

They are widespread throughout the Indo-Pacific area, and grow to a length of about three inches.

Three Spot Dascyllus—*Dascyllus trimaculatus (Pomacentridae)*. This little pomacentrid is plentiful from Hawaii, where it can be collected with ease, through the tropical Pacific into the Red Sea. Its range extends through Melanesia, Micronesia, the East Indies, and as far as Australia.

When small it is quite attractive, with its small stark white oval spots on the sides of an otherwise black body. As it grows, so do the spots until, when the fish has grown to about three inches, they are proportionately much larger.

It exhibits the pomacentrid habit of hovering around coral heads, usually in shallow water. It feeds on shrimp and crab larvae, so brine shrimp should make the ideal food. It grows to a length of about five inches.

Clown Anemonefish—*Amphiprion percula (Pomacentridae)*. There is probably no stranger relationship that exists in the seas than that between sea anemones and anemonefishes. The anemonefish lives and takes refuge among the tentacles of certain anemones, chiefly *Discoma* and *Stoichactis*. While other fish are discouraged or killed by the stinging cells of the anemone's tentacles, anemonefishes secrete a mucus which prevents the discharge of the paralyzing nematocysts.

The relationship between these two animals is mutual. In return for providing a place of refuge, the fish occasionally brings a piece of food to the anemone and keeps it groomed by nibbling at the tentacles and massaging it vigorously with thrashing movements of its tail and body. All this seems to be necessary for the anemone's survival for it will languish and die without fish to care for it.

Several observations have been made on spawnings, but unfortunately even though the eggs were hatched the young could not be raised. According to Franck de Graaf who made his observations in "Artis-Aquarium", the fish start their spawning activities by rubbing and pressing against each other, after which they start to clean a small stone near the anemone. The pre-spawning behavior and the spawning itself is similar to that of the cichlids. The eggs receive intensive care, with both male and female cleaning and aerating them. (In our picture the female is cleaning the eggs while the male is in the background). While one works the other rests in the tentacles of the nearby anemone.

The eggs are attached by a short filament, and hatch in eight days at 77 to 79°F. The young are about 5 to 5 mm long and are strong swimmers. No care is given the young after hatching and if any remain near the spawning site they are eaten by the parents. Usually a new spawn is produced four days after the young hatch out.

Amphiprion percula seems to be more at ease when surrounded by a few of its own species. Several will hover about and take refuge in the same anemone and I have seen as many as 24 nestled together among the tentacles.

Brine shrimp, both frozen and live, along with diced shellfish, should be fed to them. This can be supplemented

Bodianus rufus—Spanish Hogfish.

A. VAN DEN NIEUWENHUIZEN

Zanclus cornutus—Moorish Idol.

with dried food. A few larger pieces of clam should be provided for the fish to carry to the anemone. They range throughout the tropical Indo-Pacific Ocean.

Pink Skunk Anemonefish—*Amphiprion akallopisos (Pomacentridae)*. Like the preceding species, this fish lives in association with anemones. It does not seem to bunch up with others of its kind as the clown anemone does. Usually only one, or perhaps two, will be found in a single anemone.

Another member of this group, similar to this species, is

Zebrasoma flavescens—Yellow Tang.

the orange anemonefish, *A. perideraion*. It has a narrow white streak on the top of its head and a thin white bar on the side of the head behind the eye.

Care and feeding should be as for *A. percula*; however, both of these species are harder to acclimate to a tank and will need special attention. They are found in the tropical Indo-Pacific Ocean and grow to a length of three or four inches.

Saddleback Anemonefish—*Amphiprion laticlavius* (*Pomacentridae*). The saddleback appears to grow a little larger than any of the preceding species, but it is by no means the largest. It is rather a hardy species and seems to be one of the last to take possession of an anemone.

Two of the largest of the anemonefishes are imported and sold under the same name, tomato anemonefish. These are *A. ephippium* and *A. melanopus*. These two fish are quite similar in size, body shape, and coloration. The difference lies in the color of the pelvic and anal fins. Those of *ephippium* are orange or red, except for the anterior edges of the pelvics, which are black. In *melanopus* these fins are all black.

Care and feeding of the saddleback is as for *A. percula*.

Yellowtail Damselfish—*Microspathodon chrysurus* (*Pomacentridae*). The yellowtail damselfish is also known as the marine jewelfish. Both names are appropriate, but because the former has been accepted by the Committee of Common Names of the American Fisheries Society and the American Society of Ichthyologists and Herpetologists, it is used here as the preferred name.

The yellowtail damsel is a very lively fish in the aquarium. It is always on the move and because of this over-activity it must be fed quite often. In the sea, these fish live in association with stinging coral. It is a common occurrence to see 50 or 100 yellowtail damselfish swarming around a russet-colored coral head, dodging back and forth as they are swept around by the surge. To collect them is a lesson in patience and endurance. Quite frequently the collector has quite a few coral burns to show for his trouble.

This fish changes color slightly as it matures. The young

are dark-blue with many iridescent spots scattered around the body. The tail is clear. With age, the body color becomes brown, the spots diminish in number, and the tail turns a bright yellow.

One of the largest of the pomacentrids, this fish will grow to be a foot long, although they are seldom seen over six inches. A two-inch fish is ideal for the home aquarium. It should be fed with adult brine shrimp and given plenty of cover.

Microspathodon is a West Indian species that is also found in Florida.

Yellowtail Wrasse—*Coris gaimardi* (*Labridae*). Most aquarists never see the adult form of this pretty little fish. This is unfortunate as the adult is even more attractive than the juvenile. The young are brick-red except for five black-bordered white areas on the sides. When the fish reach a length of 3 to 3½ inches they start to lose the juvenile coloration and display their adult characteristics, the most prominent being the abruptly yellow tail.

This fish must have sand in which to burrow. The sand should be of medium mesh, not too fine, not too coarse. The fish has a small mouth and so requires small food, such as half-grown brine shrimp and ground shrimp. It is a surprisingly hardy fish, and although I have not seen one grow to its adult pattern in the aquarium, it lives for a long time. It is a peaceful fish too, and gets along well with the other tank inhabitants.

The yellowtail wrasse has a wide range in the Indo-Pacific but it is not plentiful anywhere. It reaches a length of at least one foot.

Spanish Hogfish—*Bodianus rufus* (*Labridae*). The purple and orange color pattern is constant through the juvenile and adult stages. The juveniles exhibit the same cleaning behavior as the neon goby and the cleaner wrasses of the Pacific. Larger fish seem to solicit the attentions of these little cleaners who, apparently, remove annoying external parasites.

This fish, too, must be given suitable bottom sand in

Opisthognathus aurifrons—Yellowhead Jawfish.

which to burrow. It feeds well on small pieces of fish and ground shrimp. It grows to a length of two feet; the smaller specimens of four to five inches are most suitable for home tanks. It is found in the West Indies, southern Florida, and the Keys.

Moorish Idol—*Zanclus cornutus* (*Zanclidae*). Although closely related to the surgeon fishes, the Moorish idol does not have the spines on the sides of the caudal peduncle which are characteristic of the *Acanthuridae*. Because of its beautiful colors and bizarre shape it has long been a favorite with saltwater hobbyists, even though it is a very delicate fish and difficult to maintain in the aquarium. Moorish idols are susceptible to a variety of diseases which apparently do not bother other fishes, and in addition are difficult to feed. As

A. VAN DEN NIEUWENHUIZEN

Pterois volitans—Lionfish.

delicate as they are in captivity, they seem to be just the opposite in nature. They are very abundant around Hawaii and can be seen swimming in oily polluted harbors as well as in the crystal-clear waters of the reef.

The aquarist attempting to keep this fish must be prepared to give it special attention and to nurse it along. It is particular about what it eats, but usually live brine shrimp will tempt it enough to get it started. Its teeth are adapted for grazing algae, so algae should be included in its diet if it is to survive.

A species with a wide distribution, it is found throughout the Indo-Pacific area up to the coast of Baja California. It grows to a length of eight or nine inches.

Yellow Tang—*Zebrasoma flavescens* (*Acanthuridae*). As a family, the tangs, or surgeon fishes, are the most difficult to keep alive in an aquarium. Some, however, are hardier than others, and *Z. flavescens* is among the hardiest. All fishes of this group are herbivores, that is, they eat algae and other plants. If the algae diet can be duplicated or approximated, surgeon fishes will have a better chance of surviving than if they are fed only on fish, shrimp and other animal foods.

In the public aquarium, tanks that receive a lot of natural sunlight, and which have a good growth of algae, are usually chosen for tangs. There is a definite correlation between plant growth and the longevity of tangs.

The yellow tang has, apparently, two color phases. In Hawaii it is bright yellow, as pictured here, but throughout the rest of the Indo-Pacific it is dark brown. When it is excited for any reason, a white slash, running backwards from the pectoral fins, appears on the sides. It is usually seen three to four inches in length; it ranges from Madagascar to the Hawaiian Islands.

Yellowhead Jawfish—*Opisthognathus aurifrons* (*Opisthognathidae*). One of the most "personable" fishes to enter the aquarium scene is the yellowhead jawfish. Here is a fish with a true personality. It seems to be as curious about the people on the outside of the tank as the people watching are about it.

The jawfishes are burrowing fishes; they construct tunnel-like holes, some as much as 18 inches deep. The funnel-like entrances to these burrows are usually lined with small pebbles or pieces of rock, much as a river bank is rip-rapped to prevent it from collapsing. The arrangement of the rocks never seems to be quite right and the occupant of the burrow is constantly rearranging, straightening, and substituting pieces of rubble.

These fish are habitual tail-standers, usually seen hanging almost erect over the entrances to their burrows, which they defend with vigor.

Any jawfish kept in the aquarium should be provided with deep sand and a supply of small pebbles with which to build its burrow. Several in a tank will provide hours of entertainment.

It will feed on almost anything, and therefore is an easy fish to maintain in captivity. Care must be taken to have a tight cover on the aquarium as these fish will jump out during the night, even through a surprisingly small opening.

They are found in scattered locations throughout the West Indies and Florida Keys, and grow to a length of about four inches.

Lionfish—*Pterois volitans.* This fish is known by several other names, among them turkeyfish and zebrafish. No matter what it is called, it is an extremely interesting fish and one that does well in captivity. It is one of the few salt-water fishes that shows any degree of growth, and many will outgrow one tank after another.

The lionfish is best known for the fact that its spines act as hypodermics; they eject a venom which is contained in sacs at their base; to be stung by one or more of them is quite painful. Victims report varying degrees of burning, stinging, swelling, redness and numbness. The irritation varies from mild to excruciating pain, with victims thrashing on the ground and beating the affected member against a solid object in an attempt to alleviate the agony. Hence, great care should be exercised with this species and particular caution observed when small children are around.

In spite of the fact that the lionfish can be dangerous, it becomes quite tame and learns to take food from the hand. Although live food is preferred, it will eat pieces of cut fish and shrimp.

All species of *Pterois* have large mouths and will make short work of any other tank fish small enough for them to swallow. Care should be taken to keep them with species of their own size or larger. They are found from the Red Sea through the Indo-Pacific Ocean, and grow to more than a foot in length.

Hawaiian Lionfish—*Pterois sphex (Scorpaenidae). Pterois sphex* is not nearly as spectacular or colorful a fish as the preceding species, yet it is a handsome addition to the aquarium.

Pterois sphex—Hawaiian Lionfish.

P. sphex and its smaller relative, *Dendrochirus brachypterus,* the dwarf lionfish, are quite common in Hawaii. They can be found on top of shallow reefs at night by torch lighting, or by diving down the face of a reef during the day and searching the holes and caves.

What has been said about care, feeding and compatability for *P. volitans,* is true for this species. It reaches a length of ten inches. This fish is restricted to the Hawaiian islands.

Banded Coral Shrimp—*Stenopus hispidus.* No marine aquarium is complete without an invertebrate species or two. They complete the picture of the natural community. Species must be chosen that are harmless to the fish and in turn will not be bothered themselves.

The red and white banded coral shrimp is one such species. Usually it perches on or under a rock, not moving far from its chosen place except for food. It pays little attention to the

Stenopus hispidus—Banded Coral Shrimp.

fish in the tank except to fend them off with its long delicate pinchers if they become too inquisitive.

Occasionally the empty shell of one of these shrimp will be found in the tank with its former occupant nearby. This shedding or moulting process is associated with growth. When the shrimp becomes too large for its external covering, it leaves its shell by backing out through a split which appears between the body and the tail. For several days, before its new hard shell develops, the shrimp will probably be very reluctant to put in an appearance, for in this condition it is easy even for smaller fishes to nip a leg or claw.

Coral shrimp do not need any special food as they will pick up what food the fish allow to drop to the bottom. They should be given rock overhangs or other places to hide, and water must be kept in the best condition.

They are widely scattered throughout the world in tropical water, and grow to a length of about four inches.

White Sea Anemone—*Stoichactis sp.* So flower-like are the anemones that the uninitiated find it hard to believe that these are living animals, not plants.

The anemones are related to other well-known marine invertebrate animals, such as coral, jellyfish, and the Portugese man-of-war. These are members of a group, or phylum, of the animal kingdom known as coelenterates. All coelenterates possess stinging cells or nematocysts, which are used for paralyzing and capturing their food. In most cases these nematocysts and their toxins are not strong enough to puncture or irritate human skin, but there are some exceptions: the sea nettle, stinging coral and Portuguese man-of-war. Normally one feels only a sticking or clinging sensation that is like pulling one's fingers over fine sandpaper.

Anemones are all sizes, shapes and colors, and are found all over the world. Some, such as those on the coral reefs of the South Pacific, grow to two or three feet in diameter. Others, found along the northwest coast of North America, are among the most beautiful, being found in shades of reds, pinks and greens.

Anemones must be given special care and feeding. Those of the genus *Cerianthus* should be provided with several inches of sand so that they can burrow. Most others will require a rock substratum to which they can attach themselves. These animals should be hand fed on a variety of foods. Diced clams, fish, shrimp, and whole adult brine shrimp can be offered.

Some anemones live in association with small fishes, as can be seen in the picture here. This is described in the section about Clown anemonefish.

8 Selecting healthy fish

When you pick out fish for your salt-water aquarium, you want to be sure that you are getting healthy ones. Most dealers will not knowingly sell a sick fish, but unfortunately even with the best of intentions mistakes can be made. So it is best that you know what to look for.

A healthy, strong fish will be robust and well-filled-out. Beware of the fish that has a hollow belly, or a thin pinched forehead. The body and fins should be free from any type of sore, bump, or lesion. Avoid any fish that huddles in the corner and shakes or frequently scrapes itself on the bottom or a rock. Occasional scratching is all right since a fish gets an itch now and then, the same as a human. Rubbing, scraping or scratching could very possibly mean that the fish has a parasitic or bacterial disease. Look at the fish's fins. If they are carried erect and flared, this is a good sign. Droopy fins indicate a droopy fish. If you can see the fish being fed, so much the better. A healthy fish responds to his meal with gusto.

How many fish for a tank?

Generally speaking, half as many fish can be kept in a salt-water aquarium as can be kept in a fresh-water tank of the same size. There are exceptions, of course, depending on the fish. Some species are more active than others. You will soon learn through experience exactly how many specimens your tank will support.

As a suggestion, in a 20-gallon aquarium you could put:

> 2 Clown Anemonefish
> 2 Butterflyfish
> 1 medium-sized Anemone

or:

> 1 French Angelfish
> 1 Cubbyu
> 2 Black-and-white Dascyllus
> 1 Coral Shrimp.

Sex, of course, is non-essential, as it is almost impossible for the sex of marine fishes to be determined even by exprienced keepers; and since, at the time of this writing, no marine fishes have been successfully raised in captivity, mating is of no importance.

For the beginner marine fish-keeper, either of the above groupings will make a spectacular aquarium, and provide a good start on this fascinating new hobby.

Stoichactus sp.—White Sea Anemone.